James McCosh

## Twenty Years of Princeton College

being farewell address delivered June 20th, 1888

James McCosh

**Twenty Years of Princeton College**
*being farewell address delivered June 20th, 1888*

ISBN/EAN: 9783337169442

Printed in Europe, USA, Canada, Australia, Japan

Cover: Foto ©Andreas Hilbeck / pixelio.de

More available books at **www.hansebooks.com**

# TWENTY YEARS

OF

# PRINCETON COLLEGE

# TWENTY YEARS

OF

# PRINCETON COLLEGE

BEING

## *FAREWELL ADDRESS*

DELIVERED·JUNE 20TH, 1888

BY

## JAMES McCOSH, D.D., LL.D., LITT.D.

PRESIDENT OF PRINCETON COLLEGE

NEW YORK

CHARLES SCRIBNER'S SONS

1888

# TWENTY YEARS

OF

# PRINCETON COLLEGE.

---

WELL do I remember the evening in the month
of May, 1868, in which, on coming home from my
work in Queen's College, Belfast, I found a despatch
announcing that I had been elected President of
Princeton College. The call was utterly unexpected
on my part. I felt it to be my duty to consider it,
and resisting the kind entreaties of Queen's College
and of the public, I resolved to accept the invitation
as presenting to me a wide field of usefulness, and
I wrote : " I devote myself and my remaining life,
under God, to old Princeton, and the religious and
literary interests with which it is identified, and, I
fancy, will leave my bones in your graveyard beside
the great and good men who are buried there,
hoping that my spirit may mount to communion
with them in heaven."

I spent that summer in inquiring what I should
do in my new field. I was well acquainted with
college education in Scotland, Ireland, and England;
I had visited the principal universities of Germany,

and in 1866 had travelled seven thousand miles in
the United States, and visited some of the chief
colleges and theological seminaries there.  My business now was to determine what I should make of
Princeton College, and I proceeded to draw out the
methods which I meant to pursue and embodied
them in an Inaugural Address ready for delivery.

Well do I remember the day of my arrival in
Princeton, of the welcome I received from trustees,
from the faculty, and from the students, who gave
me their tiger salute—of which I was not sure for a
few moments whether it was a welcome or a rebuke.
A few days after I got a hearty reception from the
great public interested in Princeton College, as I
delivered my Inaugural, October 27, 1868, and
published it to the world.  I hold it in my hand,
and I am quite willing that any of you should com-
pare what I then promised with what I have since
performed—with many anxieties and many imper-
fections.

It may be pleasant—yet somewhat painful—and
profitable to myself, if not to my audience, to cast
our eyes over the eventful time, now nearly twenty
years, which has passed since I entered on the office
which I am this day to resign.  The events are too
close to me to admit of my surveying them on all
sides.  I am too intimately connected with them to

be able to speak of them without deep feeling, in
which there may be not a little partiality. My
hearers will understand that in speaking of the
progress of the college I do not claim any exclusive
merit. The credit is due first to God's providence
which has favored us, and under this to trustees, to
faculty, to students, to munificent benefactors, to
innumerable friends who have prayed for us and
practically helped us—they are so many that I am
sorry to find that I have not space to name them all.
All that I claim is that I have had the unspeakable
privilege of being in all the work and in every part
of it.

I came at an opportune time. I owe any success I have had to this circumstance more than to
any other. The war so disastrous and yet so glori-
ous was over. Princeton College had suffered—not
however, in honor—but she had numerous friends,
and nobly did they gather round her, and they said,
as it were to me, in language loud enough for me to
hear, "Do you advance and we will support you."
In those days I was like the hound in the leash
ready to start, and they encouraged me with their
shouts as I sprang forth into the hunt.

When called to this place I was a professor in
the youngest of the universities set up by Great
Britain ; I had helped somewhat to form it, and in

doing so had to study the European systems
college education.  But I announced: " I have r
design, avowed or secret, to revolutionize yoı
American colleges or reconstruct them after
European model."  " I have seen enough of tl
American colleges to become convinced that the
are not rashly to be meddled with.  They are tl
spontaneous growth of your position and intell
gence ; they are associated with your history, ar
have become adjusted to your wants, and whatev
improvements they admit of must be built on tl
old foundation."

I became heir at once to a rich inheritanı
handed down by a long line of presidential ance
tors, in Dickinson, Burr, Edwards, Davis, Finle
Witherspoon, Stanhope Smith, Ashbel Green, Ca
nahan, and Maclean.  It was my privilege to rea
what others had sown ; I was awed, and yet encou
aged, by the circumstance that I had to follow suc
intellectual giants as Edwards and Witherspoo
My immediate predecessor was John Maclea...,
" the well beloved," who watched over the young
men so carefully, and never rebuked a student
without making him a friend.  But I did not allow
myself to fall into the weakness of trying to do over
again what my predecessors had done and done so
well.  My aim has been to advance with the times

and to do a work in my day such as they did in theirs.

My heart has all along been in my work, which I commenced immediately after my inauguration. I am now to give some account of that work under convenient heads. I may begin with the buildings, not because they are the most important, but because they strike the eye.

## THE BUILDINGS.

Every alumnus of the college should come up once a year if he lives not far off, and once every three years if he resides at a distance, to pay his respects to his Alma Mater, who will be sure to give him a welcome. To all who have performed this filial duty she has shown every year for the last twenty years a new building, a new fellowship, or a new professorship.

Those present at my inauguration heard the shout, sufficient to rend the heavens, when I declared that every college should have a gymnasium for the body as well as for the mind. Mr. Robert Bonner and Mr. Henry G. Marquand answered the challenge on the part of the students, and as our first benefactors engaged to raise a gymnasium, which was opened January, 1870, and the most accomplished gymnast in America appointed as superintendent.

I confess that I was disappointed when I came here with the state of the buildings. Some of the recitation rooms, especially those in the building now called the college offices, were temptations to disorder, of which the students took advantage. At times they would take out the stove, and when the class met in the morning they cried "cold," "cold," and the professor had to dismiss them; some of the instructors, however, keeping them in the whole hour. I remember one night when they took out the furniture of a room and made a bonfire of it. In these circumstances we saw the need of having new recitation rooms of a higher order, and the stately structure of Dickinson Hall, commenced in 1869, appeared completed in the campus in 1870. There the chief lectures and recitations in the academic department have been held ever since, and there from day to day an intellectual gymnasium is kept up for the strengthening of the mind. Meanwhile our students increased, and Reunion Hall, so called in honor of the reunion of the Old and New School branches of the Presbyterian Church, was begun in 1870, and finished in 1871. The library and its contents were unworthy of the college—the number of volumes was under 30,000

—and a new library building, I believe the most beautiful in the country, was finished in 1873, and the number of volumes is now toward 70,000.

All this time Mr. John C. Green was our greatest benefactor, and his brother, Chancellor Green, was always working with him. In 1873 Mr. J. C. Green started the School of Science, the most important addition which has been made to the college in my day. Since his decease, in 1875, his wishes have been carried out most honorably and generously by his trustees; the sum contributed by his estate to the good of the college must be upward of a million and a half. Of them, we in Princeton may say, in the language applied to Sir Christopher Wren, "si monumentum requiris circumspice."

These were the days of our prosperity, which was powerfully promoted by the wise counsels and the constant energies of the Hon. John A. Stewart and Mr. Henry M. Alexander, without whom I never could have done what I have been enabled to do.

In 1875 we were all touched by the gift of $15,000, left us by a very promising young man, Mr. Hamilton Murray, who perished at sea in the *Ville de Havre.* That sum was devoted by his brother to the erection of the hall which bears his

name, and which has become the College Oratory
in which prayer is wont to be made by the students,
and of which it may be said, "of this man and that
man that he was born there."

In the same year our visiting alumni would see
in Old North College the beautiful E. M. Museum,
constructed by Mr. Wm. Libbey, and arranged so
tastefully with geological specimens by Professor
Guyot.  To the same gentleman, Mr. Libbey, we
owe University Hall, erected at an expense of
nearly $200,000, first used as an hotel for the
friends of the college, and now as a dormitory
for our students.

Our numbers were increasing, and in 1876
Witherspoon Hall was built, with its elegant rooms
and grand prospect, where the students have not
only every comfort, but every means of refining
their tastes.

At this point, 1878, I have to speak with gratitude of the gift bestowed on the college and on me
by my friend the late Alexander Stuart, of the
President's house with the lovely accompanying
grounds, forming the finest residence occupied by
the president of any college in the world, and where
I have spent in comfort and elegance nine years of
my life.

In 1878–79 a telescope, provided by a few

friends, was placed in the observatory, which had been built in 1868 by General Halstead, and by it, observations have been made which let us know something of the sun and planets. In the same year houses were built for Prof. Young and Prof. Brackett, and Edwards' Hall was erected to give students rooms at a lower rate.

In 1881-82 Mr. Henry G. Marquand erected the College Chapel, the most beautiful in America, and there the members of the college will worship on Sabbath and on week days for ages to come, and draw down blessings on the college and its students in all future time.

And now you see that Biological Museum nearly completed, the noble gift of the Class of 1877, and where experiments will continually be made, by a number of our younger professors, to throw light on the mysteries of life.

As the Marquand family had done so much for Art—Mr. Frederick Marquand's trustees having given $60,000 for the endowment of a chair—I was determined that there should be an Art Museum for carrying out their intentions ; and departing from my usual practice, I went round to receive subscriptions, and raised $42,000, given in the most generous manner by about a dozen contributors. That museum is in the course of erection, and will be ready early next year to receive the fine collection of pottery and porcelain promised by Dr. W. C. Prime.

## THE GROUNDS.

I remember the first view which I got of the pleasant height on which the college stands, the highest ground between the two great cities of the Union, looking down on a rich country, covered with wheat and corn, with apples and peaches, resembling the south of England as much as one country can be like another. Now we see that height covered with buildings, not inferior to those of any other college in America. I have had great pleasure in my hours of relaxation in laying out— always assisted by the late Rev. W. Harris, the treasurer of the college—the grounds and walks and locating the buildings. I have laid them out somewhat on the model of the demesnes of English noblemen. I have always been healthiest when so employed. I remember the days, sunshine or cloudy, in April and November, on which I cut down dozens of deformed trees and shrubs, and planted hundreds of new ones which will live when I am dead. I do not believe that I will be allowed to come back from the other world to this ; but if this were permitted, I might be allured to visit these scenes so dear to me, and to see the tribes on a morning go up to the house of God in companies.

## COURSE OF STUDY.

I never looked on these buildings as constituting our chief work. I remember that some critics found fault with me for laying out too much money on stone and lime. But I proceeded on system, and knew what I was doing. I viewed the edifices as means to an end, at best as outward expressions and symbols of an internal life.

I said to myself and I said to others, We have a fine old college here, with many friends ; why should we not make it equal to any college in America, and in the end to any in Europe? The friends of the Princeton saw I was in earnest, and nobly did they encourage me. I shall never forget the substantial kindness I received at that time. I could not walk up Broadway without some one coming up to me and saying, Do not you want so and so? I will help you to get it. As he met me, Mr. John C. Green took me into a corner and told me that he meant to offer to erect a certain building, adding that " if I die before this is done, I have drawn out papers to secure its execution."

I had to consider at the beginning what would be the course of study in the college. I resolved, on the

one hand, to keep all that was good in the old
studies which had trained our fathers.   But, on the
other hand, I saw there were new branches entitled
to be placed alongside the old.   The problem with
me was to make a judicious combination of the
two.   In the winter after I entered upon my duties,
a joint committee of the trustees and of the Faculty
held a number of meetings, which ended in our
drawing out a scheme which, with important modifications and improvements, has been continued to this
day.   The increase in the number of our students
and of the branches taught will now require some
new modifications, but I hope they will run in the
same line.

ELECTIVE STUDIES.

Hitherto all the students had been required to
take the same course of study, being the good old
solid one handed down from our fathers.   But this
was felt to be irksome by many who were weary of
studying Mathematics, Latin and Greek all the four
years of their course while there were new and attractive branches of literature and science from which
they were excluded.   The principle on which we
acted was that an endeavor should be made to introduce into the college every department of true
scholarship and knowledge, taking care to leave out

all that was fictitious and pretentious. But as we projected new branches we discovered that they were so numerous that we could not impose them all without burdening the minds of the students on the one hand, or on the other making them "Jacks of all trades and masters of none." Every one sees that the day of universal scholars, such as Aristotle, Scaliger, and Leibnitz, has gone by and can never return. Not only have the physical sciences been multiplying, but all departments of philology, of historical, social, and philosophic study. Hence the necessity of allowing electives in the curriculum of study.

But we need to lay restraints on electives. Surely we are not to allow candidates for A. B. and A. M. to choose what studies they please. These two degrees have hitherto had a meaning, and it should be kept, so that those who have gained it may be recognized as scholars. An indiscriminate choice holds out a temptation, which many are not able to resist, to take the easiest subjects—say narrative history—or those taught by easy-going or popular teachers who may or may not exact systematic study. I hold that there are branches which are necessary to the full development of the mind, which every educated man ought to know. No one I think should be a graduate of a college who does not know mathematics and classics, the one to solidify

2

the reasoning powers and the other to refine the taste.

On a memorable occasion I defended Greek as an obligatory study in our colleges. Greek and Latin have been in fact the main instrument in transmitting to us a knowledge of the ancient world. Greek is the most perfect language, and contains the highest literature, of antiquity. The learned professions generally, but particularly the churches, have a special interest in retaining this tongue. Suppose it not to be required in our colleges, it would soon come not to be required in our schools, and so a large body of our students would be ignorant of it. Now suppose a student to have his heart touched by a divine power about the time when young men commonly choose their profession in life. He feels himself called on to devote himself to the work of the ministry of the Word. But in order to this he has to learn the language of the New Testament, beginning with its letters. Here an obstacle is presented which will effectively prevent many from going to the work to which they are called. It is certain that a college which does not require Greek will not prepare many to go forth as ministers or missionaries. This would be a great evil not only to the churches, but to the community generally. The devout young men who are studying for the ministry have a restraining and elevating influence in a college.

In Princeton there are certain branches which are
required of all in the Academic Apartment: Latin
and Greek; English; Oratory; Essay Writing;
French and German; Physics; Astronomy; Geology; Psychology; Logic and Ethics; Relation
of Science and Religion. Again, we have a
fixed course for every year. In the Freshman and
Sophomore years there is little or no variation allowed. But when a student has learned the rudi-
mentary branches and enters the Junior class, we
believe that he may be allowed, in addition to the
required studies, a choice, both in Junior and Senior
years, among a large number of the new subjects introduced into the colleges—additions being made to
them every year. I reckon that usually in these two
upper classes about one-half a student's time is given
to the required and the other half to the elective
studies. In choosing he may take the old branches
or he may take the new ones. The advantage of all
this is that the student may consult and gratify his
tastes—we find that an intense interest is taken by
certain students in the new studies—or the student
may elect the branch or branches fitted to prepare
him for his intended profession in life. One meaning to be a minister will probably elect some branch
of philosophy; the intending doctor will probably
take botany and zoology; and the lawyer history or
social sciences.

In both the required and in the elective courses
a college should seek to instruct students carefully
in the fundamental principles of the branch which
they are studying.    There is a loud demand in the
present day for college education being made what
they call " practical."    I believe that this is a mistake.    A well-known shipbuilder once said to me,
" Do not try to teach my art in school ; see that you
make the youth intelligent, and then I will easily teach
him shipbuilding."    The business of a college is to
teach scientific principles capable of all sorts of practical application.    The youth thus trained will start
life in far better circumstances than those who have
learned only the details of their craft, which are best
learned in offices, stores and factories, and will commonly far outstrip them in the rivalries of life.    He
will be able to advance when others are obliged to
stop ; he will be ready to take advantage of oppor-
tunities which are lost to them, and will commonly
advance the business in which he is engaged.

### FELLOWSHIPS AND PRIZES.

I have often been asked, How do the American
colleges stand in comparison with the European ones?
I believe I can answer that question.    The scholarship of the great body of the students is as high in
America as in Europe.    But they rear in Great

Britain and in Germany a body of ripe scholars to whom we have nothing equal in the New World. This led me to propose that we should institute Fellowships in Princeton College. At an early stage there were friends who established Fellowships in Mental Science, in Classics (lapsed), in Mathematics, and Experimental Science, and at a later date in Biology, each providing $600 a year to the student who stood highest in a competitive examination. Latterly some of our younger alumni have been adding University Fellowships, one in Social Science, one in Biological Science, one in English, and probably one in Philosophy, each yielding $400 or $500 a year, and open to the graduates not only of Princeton, but every other authorized college. These Fellowships have given a powerful stimulus to study, and enabled us to produce scholarship of a high order.

This may be the proper place to refer to the prizes received during my presidency : The Lynde Prize for Power of Debating ; the Alexander Guthrie McCosh Prize for Philosophic Essay ; the Baird Prizes for Oratory ; the 1876 Class Prize for a debate on Politics ; Class 1883 Atwater Prize in Political Economy ; the White Prize in Architecture.

## PROFESSORS.

When I became President, the number giving
instruction was ten professors, four tutors, two teachers, in all sixteen, beside three extraordinary lecturers. Some of the younger classes were taught
solely by tutors. I think it of importance to have a
succession of young men teaching in a college to
give fresh life to it, and out of whom to draw professors. But I believed that every class should have
at least one man of experience giving it instruction,
and it was arranged that all freshmen should be
under one or more professors. The professors then
were chiefly men of mature life, of high ability
and character. In adding new branches we had to
get new professors. It was my duty to call the
attention of the trustees to suitable persons for the
new or for the vacant offices. In doing so I looked
out for scholarly men, wherever I could hear of
them. If I found that they were not available or
not likely to promote the moral and religious welfare of the students, I thought no more of them;
and I continued to inquire till I was able to recom-
mend one whose influence would be altogether for
good. In pursuing this course we have taken several able men from other colleges.

But I have often had great difficulty in getting

a full endowment for a professor's chair—more difficulty than in getting a building. So we set ourselves
earnestly to the work of rearing professors. We
kept our eye upon our promising graduates, and
appointed them tutors or instructors, with a small
salary, and then raised them to the position of assist-
ant professors, or full professors. Thus the Board
of Trustees has chosen three professors from the class
of 1874 and six from the class of 1877. So we
have been adding new professors from year to year.
The number of professors is now thirty-five, with
three tutors and several assistants and lecturers— in
all upwards of forty. We have three professors of
Mental Philosophy, three of Greek, two of Latin, three
of Mathematics, three of English including Oratory,
two of History and Political Science, three of Modern Languages, two of Physics, two of Astronomy,
two of Chemistry, three of the Natural Sciences,
including Botany, Zoology and Geology, three of
Engineering, and two of Art. We have professors
who teach the Harmony of Science and Religion,
who teach Anglo-Saxon, who teach Oratory, who
teach Pedagogic, who teach Sanscrit, who teach
Physiological Psychology, who teach Physical Geography, who teach Anatomy and Physiology. Every
student is required every year to write a number of
essays. I am not sure that there is any college in

America which has so well an arranged system of essay writing. Princeton College has always paid attention to public speaking and we have kept this up, by requiring every student, unless incapacitated by physical weakness, to speak before a public audience. The strength of our college lies in its staff of professors. I am proud of those whom I have recommended to the trustees. We give instruction in a greater number of branches than are usually taught in the universities of England, Scotland, and Ireland, and in nearly all the branches taught in Germany.

I have pleasure in stating that the Faculty has all along stood in the most pleasant relationship towards me. I regard all the members as personal friends. I am bound to say that they watch over the interests of the college with great faithfulness.

## APPARATUS AND COLLECTIONS.

Along with the increase of professors, our friends have purchased for us a large increase of scientific apparatus. In several departments almost every new instrument of value has been provided. When I came here, the natural science collection, saving only what was done in physical geography by Dr. Guyot, was particularly defective, fit only to be turned. Now we have most valuable collections in botany and geology. For several years we have been enabled to send companies of students to make summer explorations in the West. Lying on the ground at night, they were employed all day in collecting plants and fossils, some of which are very rare and of great value. These have been placed in our museum, which is visited in consequence by many scientists.

## CONTRIBUTION TO LITERATURE AND SCIENCE.

Our professors have not only been attending to their work in the college as instructors, but have been widening the field of knowledge, each in his own department. I at one time thought of printing as an appendix to this address a list of the books, pamphlets, and articles published by our professors since I came here, but I found that it would double the size of this volume. The classical professors have been publishing text-books which are used in a number of our institutions. Our scientific teachers have been issuing volumes and papers of great value, and all of them increasing our knowledge of certain departments of nature. The *Princeton Review* has all along been conducted by Princeton editors : Dr. Hodge, Dr. Atwater, and Mr. Jonas Libbey, and now with great ability in a new form by Professor Sloane.

The valuable *Archæological Journal* is edited by one of our younger professors.

It is proper to add that the students issue three periodicals. *The Nassau Literary Magazine* has all along been an organ of a high character, and contains solid articles of superior literary ability. The *Princetonian* some years ago was in the way of attacking the Faculty. Now it is conducted in the most admirable spirit—only it gives more space to gymnastics than to literature. "Pray," said an Oxford Don to me after reading several numbers, "are you the President of a gymnastic institution?" It shows the spirit that reigns in our college that we have now a religious organ, *The Philadelphian*, containing high class articles fitted to do good among the students.

## THE SCHOOL OF SCIENCE.

Our School of Science has a body of able professors. It gives instruction in mathematics, in the various branches of physical science, and in modern languages. We seek to make its students educated gentlemen, and not mere scientists. We require Latin (or in engineering, French) on the part of those who enter. All the students receive instruction in English and write essays. To preserve them from the materialistic tendencies of the day, they are required to attend the classes either of Psychology or Logic. It is evident that this school, which has now ninety-two students, will rise every year in public estimation. Our two departments, the Academic and the Scientific, send out every year a large body of educated young men to occupy important positions all over the country.

## PHILOSOPHY IN PRINCETON.

As we added branch after branch, it was found that we could arrange them, the old and the new, into three grand departments : Language and Literature, Science, and Philosophy. We did not separate these absolutely, but we have constantly kept the distinction in view. I remember the day when Mrs. Robert L. Stuart came down to Princeton and handed me $154,000, to enable me to establish a school of philosophy.

As the head of the college, I have endeavored to give each of our varied departments its own place, and carefully to arrange a balance of studies, so as to keep the minds of the students from being one-sided, and therefore narrow and exclusive. But while I was President I became also a professor, and I am glad that I did so, for I was thereby brought into closer relationship with the students, and came to know them better.

Following my tastes, I have endeavored to create and sustain an interest in all branches of mental philosophy. I have usually been teaching three departments : Psychology, the History of Philosophy, and Contemporary Philosophy, and have branched off into Æsthetics and Metaphysics. The other two mental sciences, Logic and Ethics, have been taught by Professor Ormond and Professor Patton. I strove to make the study attractive, and have commonly had under me upwards of two hundred students, many of them elective. In connection with my classes I had library meetings in my house, in which papers were read on philosophic subjects by alumni and others and afterwards discussed by students of the upper classes, and occasionally by professors. The attendance was at first about a dozen, but it soon rose to from seventy to one hundred and fifty. Many will remember all their lives the stimulating effects of these meetings.

In my teaching I have followed the plan of the German professors, first lecturing on the subject, and after a time giving my expositions to the world in published volumes. The public has not always followed my philosophy, but has given me, what greater men than I have not been able to gain—a hearing, both in this country and in Great Britain. I am gratified to find my college lectures on Psychology and Logic (in Queen's College, Belfast) in a great many upper schools and in a number of colleges in America. Dr. Duff, the great missionary, sent me a message on his deathbed, to prepare a text-book on mental science for India, to save them from materialism diligently taught them by books from England. This I have now done in my two small volumes on Psychology, which have been sanctioned by the University of Calcutta, while steps are being taken to have them adopted in other colleges in India. Pupils of mine are using them in Japan and Ceylon. My pupils may be pleased to learn that the lectures which I delivered to them are reproduced in these distant lands. So early as my college days in Scotland, I was so ambitious as to hope that I might some day produce a work on philosophy ; little did I dream that it would be used in western America and in eastern Asia.

I am represented as being of the Scottish school of philosophy. I am not ashamed of my country, certainly not of my country's philosophy. I was trained in it. I adhere to it in one important principle : I believe that the truths of mental philosophy are to be discovered by a careful observation and induction of what passes in the mind. Not that our observation and induction gives them their authority ; they have their authority in themselves ; but it is thus we discover them. But in other respects I differ from the Scottish school. I profess to get my philosophy from the study of the human mind directly, and not from the teaching of others. The Scottish school maintains that we know only the qualities of things; I say we know the things themselves. Hamilton makes our knowledge relative; I make it positive. So I call my philosophy Realism, and by help of a few obvious distinctions I hope to establish it. America has as yet no special philosophy of its own. I long to see it have such. This must be taken directly from the study of the mind, and not from Germany or any other source. My ambition is to aid a little in the foundation of an American philosophy which, as a philosophy of facts, will be found to be consistent with a sound theology.

## POST-GRADUATE STUDENTS.

From an early period of my presidency we have had post-graduate students. We have always thrown open our doors to them. We encourage them because it is out of them we hope to make scholars. In our crowded curriculum we cannot expect in the under-graduate course of study to produce a high erudition in any one department. But when students come up to us after graduation and take up earnestly one or two departments, we can carry them on to very high attainments, and it may be prepare them to be professors. The number of our graduate students has been gradually increasing. This last year we have had seventy-eight. I have commonly had upwards of forty, most of them students from the seminary, studying the higher questions of philosophy. These graduate classes will force us on to become a university.

We have devised and published a way by which higher degrees of Doctor of Philosophy, Doctor of Science, Doctor of Literature, and Bachelor of Theology may be obtained from us by the graduates of any college, without residence, by pursuing a course of study and standing an examination. This is a measure full of promise, and I hope will be carried out when I retire. It will gather round us a body of men eagerly pursuing high studies.

### ALUMNI ASSOCIATIONS.

I think I may claim to have taken great pains to keep our graduates in close connection with the college. I have set up a great many alumni associations (there are in all eighteen), and have often visited them, travelling hundreds and some years thousands of miles for this purpose, and reporting the state of the college as I went along. I have enjoyed these meetings with the graduates, and

have returned with a most valuable knowledge of
what the community expects of the college. I proposed several years ago that the Alumni should
have authority to appoint an Advisory committee,
with power to give recommendations to the Board
of Trustees and to enter any class-room. The pro-
posal was not adopted. It may come up in some
future year.

### OUR FUNDS.

I am not to give an account of our finances, which
have been carefully watched over by Mr. John A.
Stewart and Mr. Charles Green. Some of our
friends do not let their left hand know what their
right hand doeth, and so I am not able to speak with
precision of the gifts we have received. I believe
that nearly three millions have been contributed
to the college during my tenure of office. The
principle on which we have proceeded has been
never to contract any debt and never to lay up any
money. Only on one occasion did we contract any
large amount of debt, and Mr. R. L. Stuart, who
contributed $100,000, joined some of our trustees in
paying it off. We are laboring under no debt at
this moment. But the trustees will require to cast
themselves on the friends of the college to enable
them to fulfil the obligations which they have con-

tracted on the retiring of one president and the appointment of another.

I may mention here that, to encourage struggling young men, we have funds contributed by generous friends whereby we give scholarships of $100 a year each, and $30 more if they intend to be ministers, to one hundred and seventy students. Dr. Duffield manages these funds with great care and kindness.

OUR CONTRIBUTORS.

I am sorry that my space does not allow of my mentioning the names of the many contributors to our college funds. Some of them have been referred to in the course of my narrative. I must refer to a few others. The Hon. John I. Blair has watched over our college with very great care, has endowed the chair of Geology, and has lately given $20,000 to the increase of professors' salaries. Mr. Lynde has given three prizes for excellence in debate. A gentleman who has given us only his initials has founded a Mathematical Fellowship and a large prize to the Freshman Class. Mr. Charles O. Baird has furthered oratory by his prizes to the Junior Class. We have received a most valuable set of papers on the late war from Mr. Pierson. You may notice that kind friends have enabled me to complete the work

3

begun by Dr. Maclean, and to hang up in the Museum portraits of all the presidents of the college and of other eminent men connected with it.

## OUR NUMBERS.

In consequence of the improvements of our teaching and our courses, our numbers have been slowly but gradually increasing.

| Years. | Students. | Years. | Students. |
|---|---|---|---|
| In 1867–8 | 264 | 1878–9 | 473 |
| 1868–9 | 281 | 1879–80 | 481 |
| 1869–70 | 328 | 1880–1 | 488 |
| 1870–1 | 364 | 1881–2 | 537 |
| 1871–2 | 379 | 1882–3 | 572 |
| 1872–3 | 376 | 1883–4 | 523 |
| 1873–4 | 417 | 1884–5 | 519 |
| 1874–5 | 408 | 1885–6 | 497 |
| 1875–6 | 483 | 1886–7 | 539 |
| 1876–7 | 472 | 1887–8 | 604 |
| 1877–8 | 496 | | |

It will be thus seen that our numbers have more than doubled—from 264 to upwards of 600.

## THE PROPOSED UNIVERSITY.

I think it proper to state that I meant all along that these new and varied studies, with their groupings and combinations, should lead to the formation of a *Studium Generale*, which was supposed in the Middle Ages to constitute a university. At one time I cherished a hope that I might be honored to introduce such a measure. From my intimate acquaintance with the systems of Princeton and other colleges, I was so vain as to think that out of our available materials I could have constructed a university of a high order. I would have embraced in it all that is good in our college; in particular, I would have seen that it was pervaded with religion, as the college is. I was sure that such a step would have been followed by a large outflow of liberality on the part of the public, such as we enjoyed in the early days of my presidency. We had had the former rain, and I hoped we might have the latter rain, and we could have given the institution a wider range of usefulness in the introduction of new branches and the extension of post-graduate studies. But this privilege has been denied me. I have always been prepared to contend with the enemies of the college, but I am not ready to fight with its greatest benefactors. So I retire. The college has been brought to the very borders, and I leave it to another to carry it over into the land of promise.

### BARBAROUS COLLEGE PRACTICES.

While this improvement of education was going on we had to contend against degrading college customs, some of which had come down from colonial times and were copied from the schools of Eng-

land.    There were *rakes* secretly issued by the
members of one class against the members of
another.    We had horn-sprees and foolish bonfires
kindled in the campus and the embers often en-
dangering the whole college buildings.    Worst of
all, we had the *hazing* and the *smoking* of students.
I resolved to put down these, when I found that
they had the serpent's power of prolonged life, and
that it was difficult to kill them.    I tried first of all
to make the classes condemn them, and often succeeded.    But at times we had to exercise discipline
on the offenders, who were commonly supported by
a considerable body of students.    I would not be
giving a true picture of the times unless I mentioned
one or two cases.

At that time morning prayers were held at seven,
and the students came out rubbing their eyes, with
their great-coats thrown loosely over their shoulders
and buttoning their clothes.    One morning I saw a
student with his head all " shaven and shorn."    I
called up a tutor and asked him whether the student
had had fever.    " No," said he ; " did you not hear
that he had been hazed ? "    I told him that I had not,
but added that the whole college would hear of it
before we had done with it.    Knowing that if I
called the hazed student to my house it would only
be to expose him to farther indignity, I asked a

professor to give me the use of his study and
invited the student to meet me there. When I
asked how he felt on being hazed, he replied,
" Very indignant." I said I was glad to hear it.
He told me that a company of students disguised
had come into his room late at night, that they
gagged his mouth lest he should cry and his ears
lest he should identify them ; that they had shaved
his head, then put him under the pump, and left
him tied on the campus. I asked if he had any
friends. He answered, " Few, sir ; I am a poor
Irish boy, but one man has helped me ; " naming
Chancellor Green. " My dear fellow, you have a
noble friend." I wrote a letter to the chancellor and
ordered the student to set off with it next morning
before dawn, and tell what had been done to him.
Next morning, a little after eight, I saw the noble
form of the chancellor pass my window and enter
my study. Hitherto he had been very cold toward
me—I believe he did not see the propriety of bring-
ing over a Scotchman to be the head of an American
college. He asked me somewhat sternly, " Are
you in earnest?" I answered that I was never
more in earnest in my life. " But," said he, " I
have often found when I tried to uphold the
college in putting down evils there was a weak
yielding." I told him that he might find that

this was not just my character.    He asked me
what I meant to do.    I answered that I was a
stranger, newly come to this country, that I had
asked for a conference with him—an alumnus,
a trustee, and as the head of the law in New
Jersey—to ask his advice.    " Can you not," said he,
" summon the perpetrators before the faculty ? "
"Yes," I replied, " but I have little evidence to
proceed on.    The student thinks he knows two of
those who gagged him, but is not sure ; and students capable of such deeds reckon it no crime to
lie to the faculty."    " What then are we to do ? "    I
replied that I wished him to say.    But he again
asked, " Are you in earnest ? "    I said " he might
try me."    He then proposed that we should start
a criminal process, and said he would engage the
attorney-general as prosecutor, and would see that
the jury was not packed.    I said, " I accept your
terms," and added, " You may now go home, Chancellor, the case is settled."    He asked, " What do
you mean ? " looking at me with amazement.    I
simply mentioned that I had been dealing with students for sixteen years, and knew that the case was
settled.    I felt that the time was come when I
should be as cold to him as he had been to me.    I
thanked him for coming to me when I meant to go
to him, and bade him good-morning.    I asked a

professor to send for one of the students supposed to have been guilty, and to tell him that the great chancellor had been here, that he was that day to engage the attorney-general as prosecutor, and that if the guilty parties did not send me an apology in forty-eight hours they would all be in prison. In a few hours I received a humble letter, signed by about a dozen students, confessing that they were guilty, expressing their sorrow, and promising that they would never commit a like offence. I sent a message to the professors, asking them to be in their place next morning at prayers, and the students were prepared for something to come when they saw them all assembled. I took out the paper sent me, and read it till I came to the signatures, when I put it in my pocket, saying, " I accept the apology and the promise, and neither the faculty nor any other shall ever know the names. Let us read the passage on repentance, 2 Cor. vii." I never saw the college more moved.

For some years hazing was considerably subdued. But it continued in other colleges which have not had the courage to grapple with it, and has reappeared in this college once and again and has led to some very painful scenes. It has for the present disappeared, I trust finally.

As a happy consequence of this act I gained

the friendship of Chancellor Green, who ever afterwards stood by me in the Board of Trustees and beyond it, telling those who opposed my measures that in opposing me they would have to oppose him. His family became deeply interested in the college, and have been our most generous benefactors. I was gratified when his family asked me to be a mourner at the funeral of that man, one of the greatest that Jersey has produced.*

I may state that this was the first and last case in which I resolved to carry discipline into a criminal court. I thought it right to let the college know that the criminal courts could interfere in such a case. But it is better that the faculty should exercise discipline in a paternal spirit. Another incident may be given. A company resolved to *smoke* a student. They entered his room vigorously puffing out tobacco fumes, hoping thereby to sicken him. The faculty sent them home to their fathers and mothers. At the close of one of my Bible recitations about twenty students remained behind and asked to speak with me, and they spoke feelingly of the pain which the dismissal of their companions would give to fathers

---

* Mr. Courtland Parker said to me as we rode in the same carriage at his funeral, "When the Chancellor summed up the evidence and addressed the criminal condemned to die, I always felt that I had a picture of the day of judgment."

and mothers and grandmothers. I saw at once that
I had before me, not those who had been engaged
in the foul deed, but the best students in the class,
who had been elected as most likely to have an influence over me. It occurred to me that I might catch
them in the trap which they had laid for me. I said
to them, " Do you approve of the deed which has been
done ? " " No." they answered heartily. " But how,"
I asked, " do you propose to stop such acts ? " They
were staggered. I saw out of the window two hundred students gathered like a thunder-cloud on the
campus and threatening rebellion. I said, " Gentlemen, go out to these students and ask them to pass a
resolution condemning the offensive practice ; " and I
promised that if they did so I would ask the faculty
to rescind their sentence. To show that I was not
afraid, I passed by the crowd on my way home and
heard a student denouncing the abominable deed
that had been committed by the students. The
company was divided and soon scattered. They
had planned on that afternoon to rise in a body and
leave the chapel. No one rose, and the threatening
cloud passed away.

When these *emeutes* took place we were always
favored with the visits of interviewers from the New
York newspapers. I remember that one day when
I was coming down from New York, I had a dozen

reporters on the same train, all bent on carrying back a sensational story founded on some small disturbance which had occurred the night before. At one of these times a reporter from a reputable journal called on me for information. I told him that I would give him this, but that he must publish what I said to him, which he agreed to do, and I began : "Whereas a certain newspaper," naming it, "had been publishing vile stories against Princeton College, evidently written by sub-editors from a rival college, the alumni and students of Princeton were about to form a combination in which each member binds himself never to buy a copy of that paper." The reporter wrote a while, and then put his pen behind his ear and said, "President, this will never do," and promised to speak to the editor ; and in a day or two after the editor wrote me, asking me to appoint a reporter from among the students, and we were troubled no more from that quarter.

I mention these things in order to give me an opportunity of explaining that these scenes of disturbance, which were reported years ago in so exaggerated a form, almost always rose from our putting down debasing customs. I could not in dignity answer the distorted reports, and many believed them. We have now happily put down all these old barbarous customs, and of late years I have no complaint to make of the newspaper press. It seems inclined to speak good of us rather than evil, and of myself, I am sure it praises, vastly more than they deserve, the efforts I have made for the advancement of the college.

I do not wish to fight old battles over again, but if I am to give a correct account of the period, I must mention the important historical events.

## SECRET SOCIETIES.

When I became connected with Princeton, the secret Greek Letter Fraternities had considerable power in the college. The trustees years before had passed a law requiring every entering student to come under a solemn obligation to have no connection whatever with any secret society. I felt from the beginning that the college was in this respect in a very unhappy position, the students signing a pledge which a number of them knowingly violated. On inquiry I discovered that while some of the societies did mean to foster pleasant social feelings and to create a taste for oratory, yet that their influence was upon the whole for evil. I soon found that the societies sought to get the college honors to their members and to support those who were under college discipline. I felt that as the head of the college I must put an end to this state of things.

I was powerfully aided or rather led in carrying this out by the late Dr. Atwater, who had more credit than I in suppressing the secret societies. One courageous student set himself vigorously to oppose the attempt to get the college honors to members of the fraternities. The difficulty was to get evidence. But certain lodges got photographs taken of their members. These fell into our hands. The offenders stood clearly before us. I summoned them before the faculty. They did not deny the charge and we sent them home. In a short time each sent in a paper in which he promised to give up while in college all connection with secret societies. I retained these papers for a time to secure that the promise should be kept, but I have shown them to no one. The faculty restored the students, who, I believe, kept their word. Now the great body of the students would earnestly oppose the reintroduction of these fraternities into our college. Most of the professors in the American colleges profess to lament the existence of such societies, but have not the courage to suppress them. I am sorry to find that of late some eminent men belonging to other colleges have been defending these secret organizations.

One of the greatest evils arising from the Greek letter societies is that they tended to lessen the numbers and usefulness of our two noble societies, the

Whig and the Cliosophic. These form an essential part of our educational system. They have done as much good as any other department of our college teaching. They have helped mightily to prepare our young men for the pulpit, the bar, and the senate. I may be permitted to suggest that the barbarous customs at entrance might be profitably abandoned. I farther think that the societies should be so opened that from time to time each should have great public debates open to ladies as well as gentlemen. Not till then can we have the highest style of popular eloquence.

## GYMNASTICS.

I feel a great pride in remembering that I introduced gymnastics into the college. The sentence of my Inaugural in which I declared that there should be exercises in the colleges to strengthen the bodily frame called forth loud acclamations. Since that time gymnastics have had an important place under careful superintendents and our students have manfully kept their own. From the gymnastic exercises within our walls and grounds much good has arisen and no evil. The bodily frames of our students have been strengthened, and their health sustained by the manly exercises, while habits of mental agility and self-possession have been acquired, of great use in preparing young men for the active duties of life.    .

But there may be, there have been, evils arising from the abuse of competitive games, especially with professionals.  The applause given may create an enthusiasm which should rather be directed to study.  Some may prefer the approving shout of ten thousand spectators on the ball field to the earning of a class honor or a university fellowship.  The youth who can skilfully throw a ball may be more highly esteemed than one of high scholarship or character.  Your strutting college heroes may consist of men who have merely powerful arms and legs.

It is acknowledged that some of our greatest gymnasts have been as scholarly and pious as any members of their class.  There is no necessary or even usual connection between gymnastic eminence and immorality.  But there may be some half-dozen or ten in each class of a hundred who devote so much time and mind to the games that they neglect their studies and virtually lose their college year. The games may be accompanied with betting and drinking.  They may tend in some cases to produce the manners of a bully or a jockey rather than of a scholar or a cultivated gentleman.  The talk of the students in the campus may be more about the nice points of football, or baseball, than of literature or science. The style of gaming may become professional instead of being promotive of health, and the great body of the students, instead of joining in the exercises, may stand by and look idly on others playing.

The question presses itself upon us, How are we to get the acknowledged good without the accompanying evils? The question is keenly discussed; I hope it will continue to be discussed till it is satisfactorily settled. Twice have I made the attempt to bring the principal Eastern colleges to an agreement. The colleges were willing to unite except one or two who trade upon their gymnastic eminence to gain students. As these stood out nothing could be done. But things have come to a crisis. Harvard and Yale now profess to see the evils that arise from competitive games. Let the discussion continue. Let it be publicly conducted. Let it be known what position each college takes. Let fathers and mothers say what they wish for their sons. Let the public press speak boldly. The issue within the next year or two will be that we shall have the good without the evil. Meanwhile let Princeton proclaim that her reputation does not depend on her skill in throwing or kicking a ball but on the scholarship and the virtue of her sons.

## THE MORALITY OF THE COLLEGE.

If any one tells me that in a college with hundreds of students there is no vice he is either deceived himself or is endeavoring to deceive others. We acknowledge that there are evils in our college, but we do all we can to repress them. Of late years there has been very little vicious conduct in Princeton College. What exists is obliged to hide itself. The great body of the students discountenance it, and do not, as they were often tempted to do in former years, defend those who may be under discipline.

I hold that in every college the Faculty should look after, not only the intellectual improvement, but the morals of those committed to their care by parents and guardians. I am afraid that both in Europe and America all idea of looking after the character of students has been given up by many of our younger professors. Their feeling is, " I am bound to give instruction in my department and to advance the study in all quarters ; but as to looking after the private character of any student, I do not recognize it to be part of my duty and I shrink from it, I decline to undertake it." I have been very careful not to let this spirit get abroad among our young instructors. Our law enjoins that every professor is bound in duty to watch over the welfare of the students, many of whom are far from home. We have a tutor or officer in every college building whose office it is to see that those living there conduct themselves properly.

We have abandoned 'the spy system, and our officers do not peep in at windows or through key-holes—a practice at which the student would generally contrive to outwit his guardian. With us everything is open and above board. We proceed on the principle that the college stands *loco parentis*. The youth is treated as he would be by a parent. We listen patiently to every one against whom a suspicion is entertained or a charge brought. We dismiss no one without evidence, and there is rarely if ever a case in which the culprit does not confess his guilt. Our penalties consist in sending home the youth for a shorter or longer time to his parents, that they may deal with him.

For sixteen years I had the somewhat invidious task of looking after the morals and discipline of the college. Since that time this important work has been committed to Dean Murray, who has shown more patience than I did in the discharge of his duties. Parents may be satisfied when they know that he is looking after the best welfare of their sons.

I could weep this day, did I not restrain myself,

4

over some who have fallen when with us. But I am able to say that when parents join with us in the exercise of discipline, it commonly succeeds in accomplishing its end, the reformation of the offender. We have the privilege and the advantage of a great many of the youths sent us having been well trained at home. I am able to testify that God has been faithful to his promise, "Train up a child in the way he should go, and in his old age he will not depart therefrom."

There is a much more pleasant relationship between the professors and the students of late years. It is a much easier thing now to govern the college. This is especially so since a provision has been made for a conference between the Faculty and an elected committee of the students as to judicial cases. I doubt much whether such a measure could have been made to work beneficially in some earlier years, as the students might have chosen representatives to fight with the Faculty. This conference, long contemplated by me, has been carried into effect by Dean Murray with the happiest results.

I believe the moral tone of the college is upon the whole sound at this present moment. Lately the students, with my consent and approval, held a mass-meeting and denounced the base men who send them obscene publications by mail. At the same meeting they voted unanimously for No License in this town, and helped greatly in carrying this measure in the burgh. I cannot tell how happy I am to think that when I give up my office in the college, there is not a place for the sale of spirituous liquors in all Princeton.

## RELIGION IN THE COLLEGE.

From the beginning Princeton has been a religious college professedly and really. It has given instruction weekly on the Bible, and required attendance at prayers daily and on public worship on the Sabbath. The prayers in the chapel are conducted by the President and professors in their turn, and the preaching by those of us who are ministers, and very frequently now by eminent divines who are invited to visit us. Dean Murray conducts public worship with great acceptance once a fortnight. Our Sabbath services of late years are not found to be tedious by the students. Every Sabbath afternoon at five there is a meeting of the whole college for prayer, and a ten-minutes address which is commonly interesting as well as useful.

There is much talk in certain quarters of the importance of giving instruction in the English Bible in colleges. Let me tell those who are recommending this to us, that this has always been done

in Princeton. We are not ashamed, neither professors nor students, of the gospel of Jesus Christ.

In entering upon my work here I found some difficulty in inducing those who had previously conducted religious instruction to continue to do so, so
I undertook the whole work myself. For eight
years I gave Bible instruction weekly to every student. My course lasted four years, and in these I
carried the students in a general way through the
Bible.

I am not sure that I acted wisely in undertaking
all this work. At the end of the eight years I
divided the work among several others, reserv-
ing always to myself an important part, the Penta-
teuch and the Epistle to the Romans, on which the
seniors were required to recite. Latterly I have
given up the whole Bible instruction to seven or
eight others. Dean Murray gives instruction to the
seniors in the doctrinal teachings of the gospels and
the epistles. Professor Ormond goes through the
book of Acts with the juniors. Professor Orris takes
up St. John's Gospel in Greek with the Academic
sophomores and Professor Winans takes up St.
Luke's gospel. The Academic freshmen are taken
over a general introduction to the study of the Scrip-
tures, the poetical books of Scripture and the par-
ables of our Lord by Professors Hunt, West, and

Tutor Roddy. Professor Macloskie gives two courses to the sophomores and freshmen in the School of Science—one on lessons from the Old Testament, the other on the Life of Christ. Professor Winans has an optional class once a week, in the evening, in which he gives special instruction in the Greek of the New Testament.

The majority of the students have always been professors of religion. One year there were two-thirds, and this year there are three-fifths. I am able to testify that these students as a whole, and with some human infirmities, live consistently with the profession which they make. At this present time we have 365 names on the roll of the Philadelphia Society, which is the special religious association of the college, and which has been the centre of the spiritual life among us for many years.

We have had our times of gracious revival. I remember one year which began with a season of great religious apathy. The number attending our prayer-meetings was very small—perhaps twenty or thirty. But we had a few devoted men, some of whom had come from another college, who prayed as earnestly as ever men prayed, saying to God that " we will not let thee go except thou bless us." One night there was heard in our campus the noise of a company, who had been drinking. We summoned

before the faculty a number of students, whose names
had been called as they were returning to their
rooms. We had difficulty in making them confess.
After dealing for more than an hour with one young
man—now a lawyer in high standing—in which he
continued parrying me off, he burst out : " President,
I can stand this no longer. I was drinking, and I
fear I am getting fond of drink." We sent the band
home for a time. They returned deploring their
conduct. Our act of discipline was blessed by God.
The college was moved, many betook themselves to
prayer. Prayer meetings were numerous and earnest. Dozens were converted and have ever since
continued steadfast in the faith.

In 1876, we had a deep religious revival. Meetings for conference and prayers were held by the students every day and every night. Every student,
indeed every member of the college, felt awed and
subdued. It was estimated that upwards of one hundred were converted. I know that the great body
of them, if not all, have continued faithful, are leading consistent lives, and doing good over wide
regions in this land and in others. On one occasion some strange fire mingled at times wtih the fire
from off the altar of God. There was a jealousy
of the faculty on the part of a number of the students.
Some of the strangers who came here to address

them kept studiously away from the President and professors, lest it should be thought that the work was a scheme of the college authorities. But the few evils that appeared were overwhelmed and lost sight of in the midst of the good that was done. When the excitement was somewhat dying down, the students felt the need of the wise counsel of their college instructors, and came to put confidence in them.

In later years the religious interest has not so often taken the form of what is called a revival. But all along we have had, every year or two, seasons of deep religious earnestness, as in 1870, in 1872, in 1874, in 1882, in 1886. At the beginning of this year we had such a time on the occasion of the visit of Professor Drummond and two professors from the University of Edinburgh. At these times the meetings for prayers were frequent and well attended, and there were short meetings for worship conducted by students in the college entries about nine at night, to which all students in the entry were invited. On these occasions pains were taken to secure that every student, especially those who had made no profession of religion, were spoken to about the state of their soul. It may be said truly that no student has left our college without the way of salvation having been made known from the pulpit on the

Sabbath, by the weekly Bible instruction of professors, and by the repeated personal appeals of his
pious fellow students.

In 1877 a convention was held in Louisville for
the purpose of organizing societies for Christian
work in every college.  One of our professors, Dr.
Libbey, was induced to become a leader in this
movement.  He and Mr. Wishard, a student of ours,
engaged as secretary, visited a great many of the
colleges of the country and succeeded in establish-
ing Christian associations in them.  These ever
since have been the centres of religious life, and have
great influence in promoting religion in the colleges.
By means of them the colleges can combine to
further any good cause.  They are in friendly relationship with the Young Men's Christian Association of
America.

In 1886 two of our students, Mr. Wilder and Mr.
Forman, sons of missionaries, being stimulated by
residing in the summer in Northfield under Mr.
Moody, resolved to visit the colleges in New
England, Canada and the Middle States in order to
engage students, young men and women, to devote
themselves to the work of the Lord as missionaries
in the foreign field.  They succeeded in getting no
fewer than twenty-five hundred to profess their
readiness to go where Christ might require.  This

is, I believe, a genuine work. At this present time there is a very deep interest, greater than has ever been before, in foreign missions among the students of the college and seminary. A meeting for prayer is held after the morning service in the chapel, attended by about thirty persons, all purposing to go abroad as missionaries. A year ago the college students raised the funds to pay a missionary, and Mr. Forman has been sent out as Princeton College missionary to India.

Princeton College, during my presidency, has sent out at least three hundred men as ministers or preparing for the ministry. I know of at least twenty-five missionaries sent out during the same period to the foreign field.

Thank God we have had scarcely any avowed infidelity among us. Not above half a dozen out of our two thousand and more students have left us declaring that they had no religious belief. Several of this small number have since become decided Christians. The truth which had been addressed to them here stuck as a barbed arrow in their hearts till God gave them relief. One young man while here had set himself against all religion. Three years after graduation he was elected to deliver the master's oration, and he came back among us to give a noble defence of the truth. On another occasion, I

sent for a young man who had just graduated, of
whom I feared that he had no religious faith.   After
talking with him seriously, I asked if he would allow
me to pray with him.   He declined, saying that he
did not believe in a God to whom to pray.   So we
parted.   I had hope of him, knowing that he had a
pious mother.   I gave him a letter which helped him
to get a government position in Washington.   Some
years after, I had occasion to deliver some lectures
in Cincinnati, and was living in a hotel there.   A
stranger, who turned out to have graduated at Princeton before my day, came up to me and asked, " How
is it that you make infidels in Princeton ? "   I
answered that this was not just our vocation.   He
then began to tell me of a young man who lived in
the same boarding-house with him in Washington
who had been an open-mouthed infidel, perpetually
quoting Huxley and Spencer, and avowing himself
an agnostic.   I guessed who the young man was at
once.   After keeping me in a state of anxiety for a
time, he said that he might be able to report something that would gratify me, and he told me that
this young man had gone to his mother to con-
vert her ; "but," he added, "she floored him," and
now he is a member of a Young Men's Christian
Association, and is delivering addresses on religion.
Not long after, this youth called on me with his

newly-married wife.   On the same chair on which
he was seated when he declined to pray with me,
he now asked me to pray with him.   He is now
a minister of the Gospel, and when I saw him last
he was purposing to become a missionary.   I pray
that there may be a like issue in the case of the
few who are still wandering.

Happily I have never had any difficulty in dealing
with students on the religious question.   I have had
under me Catholics as well as Protestants of all de-
nominations, Jews and heathens.   I have religiously
guarded the sacred rights of conscience.   I have
never insisted on any one attending a religious service to which he conscientiously objected.   With
scarcely an exception, the students have attended our
daily morning prayers in the chapel, and also our
weekly religious instruction.   We allow them to go
to their own place of worship on the Sabbath.   The
Episcopalians have a St. Paul's Society, which we
encourage.   It is an interesting fact that during all
my presidency no one has left the Presbyterian
Church while in college to join any other communion.

In the instruction we give by lectures and recitations, we do not subject religion to science.   But
we are equally careful not to subject science to religion.   We give to each its own independent place,
supported by its own evidence.   We give to science

the things that belong to science, and to God the things that are God's. When a scientific theory is brought before us, our first inquiry is not whether it is consistent with religion, but whether it is true. If it is found to be true, on the principle of the induction of Bacon, it will be found that it is consistent with religion, on the principle of the unity of truth. We do not reject a scientific truth because at first sight it seems opposed to revelation. We have seen that geology, which an age ago seemed to be contrary to Scripture, has furnished many new illustrations of the wisdom and goodness of God, and that the ages of geology have a wonderful general correspondence with the six days of the opening of Genesis. It will be remembered that the late Dr. Stephen Alexander defended Kant and Laplace's theory of the formation of the earth (substantially true, though it is now shown that it has overlooked some agencies at work), which was supposed to be inconsistent with religion. I have been defending Evolution, but in doing so, have given the proper account of it as the method of God's procedure, and find that when so understood it is in no way inconsistent with Scripture. I have been thanked by pupils who see Evolution everywhere in nature because I have so explained it that they can believe both in it and in Scripture. I believe that whatever

supposed discrepancies may come up for a time between science and revealed truth will soon disap-
pear, that each will confirm the other, and both tend
to promote the glory of God.

CLOSE.

During all this time a careful Providence has
been watching over us. We have had no fire or
flood to devastate us. The health of our students
has been remarkably good. There have scarcely
been any deaths within our walls. In making this
statement I have to mention one sad exception. If
I did not restrain myself I would weep as I think of
it. In 1880, seven or eight young men were taken
away by malignant fever. I do not feel as if I were
specially to blame, as the sanitary arrangements
were not committed to me ; but we college authorities were so far to blame, and I am afraid that we
have scarcely made · atonement by immediately
after, at a large expense, making the sanitary con-
dition of the college thoroughly satisfactory. For
hours day and night was I employed in visiting the
dying, and comforting their parents. The thought
of these weeks is the most painful remembrance of
my Princeton life.

I am led, this day, to look back on my past life
in Princeton. I believe I can say truly that I have

coveted no man's silver or gold.  The little I have
laid up for old age I owe to a revered father who
cultivated the land in Scotland, and to a beloved
son, whose remains I have laid in your graveyard,
expecting at no distant day to have my own laid
beside them.  I owe no man anything, but love to
all men, gratitude for the favors bestowed on me—
far greater than any I have bestowed on others.  I
trust I have lived for a higher end than riches, or
power, or fame.  For sixteen years I was a labori-
ous minister of the Gospel, having in one of the
churches I served upwards of 1,400 communicants.
For the last thirty-five years I have been instruct-
ing young men, and in Princeton have commonly
had each year 200 young men studying philosophy
under me.  For all this I have to give account to
God.

I trust I have not been unmindful of the injunc-
tion to be "given to hospitality."  My income, happily we may suppose, did not admit of my giving
extravagant entertainments ; but when college duties
did not prevent, I often asked the fathers and
mothers of students—quite as frequently the poor
as the rich—to come to my house, and in this way I
became acquainted with the families of many of the
young men.  From time to time I had class recep-
tions, in which the students were brought into closer

relationship with one another, with my family, and the people of the town. By these means I have sought in a small way to make college life less monastic and exclusive, and to cherish pleasant social feelings. In this respect, and in every respect, I have been aided by Mrs. McCosh, provided to be my comfort, and who is appreciated by the students as being their friend in health and in sickness.

It would be altogether a mistake for any one to suppose that the life of a college president is a dull or monotonous one. If he has any life in himself, he will be interested in the whole life of the college —and no institution has more life than a college. The students feel this in the recitation rooms, in their own rooms, on the campus, and at their games ; and why should not the president's heart beat responsive to theirs ? There is something happening every day, almost every hour of the day, to call forth feeling ; sometimes, I admit, of disappointment or sorrow, more frequently of hope and joy, as notice is brought of the success of this or of that young man. There is the father and mother presenting their boy, their hearts trembling with anxiety, while the youth is wondering at what is to happen. I have been liable every hour to have calls made upon me. It is a mother asking how her son is doing, and is so pleased when I can report favorably. It is a student waiting on me to consult about his studies or his financial difficulties, to ask me to help him to get a certain position, or to tell me of the death of a father or sister. I was never disturbed by such calls. I often gathered a considerable amount of knowledge from them. The callers never stayed too long or annoyed me by improper requests. I have found when I was following some deep philosophic theme, and had run aground, that I was relieved by a student coming in to divert my thoughts, and I returned to my studies to find the difficulties gone. I have rejoiced when I found any young man advancing in his studies, particularly when he was eagerly pursuing some high branch. I confess that I scarcely know what to do with myself after I am separated from these interesting associations and employments on which so much of my happiness has depended these many years.

For the last thirty-five years my intercourse has been chiefly with young men. My heart has been in my work, and I have delighted to lecture to them, to listen to the questions they put to me when they were perplexed about some of the deeper problems of philosophy or religion. Two circumstances so far help to reconcile me to the position I have now to take.

The first, that I am to be succeeded by one in whom I have thorough confidence that he will carry on the work which has been begun ; no, but that he will carry on a work of his own. Possessed of the highest intellectual powers, he will devote them all to the good of this college. With unrivalled dialectic skill he will ever be ready to defend the truth. I am not sure that we have in this country at this moment a more powerful defender of the faith. Carrying at his side a sharp two-edged sword, he uses it only against error. I can leave with confidence these young men to his care, believing that he will watch carefully over their training in knowledge, in morals, and in religion. I am particularly happy when I think that philosophy, and this of a high order, and favoring religion, is safe in his hands, and will be handed down by him to the generation following. I feel that I will have to say, "What have I done in comparison of you ? Is not the gleaning of the grapes of Ephraim better than the vintage of Abiezer ? "

Secondly, I am pleased to find that I have still some place in this college. I should like to bring forth some " fruit in old age." My life has had two sides ; one employed in thinking, and the other in action ; and I have not found the two inconsistent. I am sure that the metaphysics I have taught have

5

been all the wiser, because I have become acquainted with men and manners.    I have been
identified with important public events in Scotland,
in Ireland, and now in the higher education in
America, and I should like to leave some record
behind of what I have done and seen, especially in
helping to form in the district in which I lived the
Free Church of Scotland.    But if I am spared to do
any important work, it must be in a different field.

I cherish the belief that God has given me some
things farther to say on the subject of philosophy,
fitted to form a basis to truth in this age of unsettled
opinion among so many young men.    I have had
the unspeakable privilege and pleasure of expound-
ing philosophy to between two and three thousand
young men in Princeton.    The lectures I delivered
here being published, have got an entrance into
India, Japan, and Ceylon.    I mean to follow this
leading of Providence.    Next winter I intend to give
here a course of very carefully prepared lectures on
First or Fundamental Principles, and immediately
after to publish them to the world, to travel as
widely as God may open ways for them.    These
will contain in epitome the results of my thoughts
for the last half century.    It is thus I mean to
employ my remaining life, be it longer or be it
shorter.

It is not without feeling that I take the step which I now take. It recalls that other eventful step in my life, when I gave up my living, one of the most enviable in the Church of Scotland, when the liberties of Christ's people were interfered with. I am sorry to be separated from the employments in which I have had such enjoyment. I regret that I no longer stand in the same relation to all the students of this college. I may feel a momentary pang in leaving the fine mansion, which a friend gave to the college and to me—it is as when Adam was driven out of Eden. I am reminded keenly that my days of active work are over.

But I take the step firmly and decidedly. The shadows are lengthening, the day is declining. My age, seven years above the three score and ten, compels it, Providence points to it, conscience enjoins it, the good of the college demands it. I take the step as one of duty. I feel relieved as I take it.

I ask forgiveness of God and man for any offence I have given in my haste. I leave with no unkind feeling toward any. I should be sorry if any one entertained a malignant feeling toward me. It has been a high honor and an unspeakable privilege, that I have been at the head of this noble institution for such a length of time, and that so many spheres of usefulness have been thrown open to me.

I leave the college, thanks be to God and man, in a healthy state, intellectually, morally, and religiously. I leave it with the prayer, that the blessing of Heaven and the good will of men may rest upon it, and with the prospect of its having greater usefulness in the future than even that which it has had in the past.

www.ingramcontent.com/pod-product-compliance
Lightning Source LLC
Chambersburg PA
CBHW021514090426
42739CB00007B/613